Flipping 101:
The Formula to Low-Risk, Profitable Flips

Flipping 101:

The Formula to Low-Risk, Profitable Flips

Chris Bello

Less dreaming, more doing.

Copyright © 2017 Chris Bello

All rights reserved. No part of this book may be used or reproduced in any manner whatsoever without the written permission of the Author. Printed in the United States of America. For information, please visit www.chrisbello.com.

I dedicate this to my parents. You have always supported my decisions whether you have liked them or not (from allowing me to play my drum set for hours as a kid to accepting my decision to jump out of planes countless times). Thanks, mom and dad.

CONTENTS

Welcome to Flipping 101 7

Chapter 1: Finding Prime Flipping Items 9

Chapter 2: Price Check Before Purchasing 14

Chapter 3: Selling Your Items 17

Chapter 4: Order Fulfillment 23

Chapter 5: Tracking Profits and Progress 27

Chapter 6: Negotiation Tips 29

Chapter 7: Ready, Set, Flip 35

About the Author 39

<u>This book is for you if you:</u>

• Would like to potentially make relatively easy money with low inventory investment costs

• Are willing to put in honest effort and a little bit of your time

<u>This book is *not* for you if you:</u>

• Use the "I don't have time" excuse often

• Think that going to discount stores or sales is beneath you

• Do not have reliable transportation to source items and bring them back to your residence or warehouse

Welcome to Flipping 101

Flipping (verb): the act of buying something at a low price and selling it at a higher price for profit.

When you see the above definition of flipping (also known as reselling), you might think, "well duh, buy low and sell high, everybody knows that." Let me ask you a few questions... what items would you flip? Would you flip cell phones? Or watches? Or maybe real estate?

Once you decide on something to flip, how would you go about finding great deals in whatever category you're searching in? You are probably starting to see how there is far more depth to this topic than you may have initially thought.

People flip all sorts of things. As the middleman, you help link products to interested buyers. The secret is sourcing your items from sellers who are basically giving them away for pennies on the dollar, far below market value. After you stock up on these items, you can simply mark them up, post them for sale, and pocket the profit once you find interested buyers.

There are books out there on how to flip real estate and big-ticket items. However, with a lot of those higher reward flips come higher risks as well. Sometimes, significant investments are necessary and you may end up sitting on inventory for longer than expected.

In this book, I'm going to be focusing on the low-hanging fruit, the easy wins that don't involve much risk at all in terms of upfront investment necessary. I'm talking about spending $25 on an item and selling it for $120 within a week. I have done so many flips like this that I've lost track. I'll teach you the exact methods I used to maximize my profits while minimizing my money and time invested.

Chapter 1: Finding Prime Flipping Items

Garage and Estate Sales

When I first decided I wanted to get into this game, I thought about how I could find cheap items of value. I had heard of people attending auctions and buying expensive equipment at huge discounts, but I wanted to start off by checking out standard, household items that could be found at garage and estate sales. The first question I typed into Google was "how do I find sales in my area?" Some site popped up that had a few addresses of local garage or estate sales, but it didn't seem like a whole lot people used it.

I had used Craigslist several times before when searching for items of interest, but I hadn't initially realized that there is a Garage Sale section. Once I discovered that, I noticed that a lot of people were actually posting sales on there. I'm talking 10-15+ sales within 20 miles of my house on multiple days of the week.

If you live in a big city or town like I do, you'll see several sales each week. This may be a little more difficult for you if you're in a tiny city where Joe Bob is the closest neighbor and lives 10 miles away. I live in Houston, Texas, where there are millions of residents in the Greater Houston area. There are surrounding suburbs that basically count as part Houston such as The Woodlands, Katy, Sugar Land, and Cypress.

A huge fraction of the population is always moving into, out of, or around the city at any given time, which means that they are also buying or selling all kinds of things. This is where the magic happens, and where you'll find the greatest opportunities.

A lot of garage sales happen when families want to do "spring cleaning." You'll find good items here sometimes, but the really good deals come from the sales where the owners are moving. The owners are literally selling their home and moving within a few months or weeks to another city, state, or possibly even country. They can't take all their stuff with them. They may be willing to sell you a really nice TV for $50 that they paid $400 for 2 years before. See where you swoop in for the deal?

Estate sales tend to happen due to downsizing, divorce, or most often from what I've seen, when a homeowner passes away. I've attended several of these, and literally everything is on sale in the entire house, even bars of soap. It's kind of crazy to see.

I went to one sale where a man's wife had passed away. Based on the size of his house and the quality of his possessions, he appeared to be extremely wealthy. Beautiful art from around the world decorated the walls. The man was literally selling everything, purchasing an RV, and planned to travel across the United States.

This was a powerful message for me. It really went to show me that "you can't take it with you." I have always been a fan of "experiences over things," and this situation solidified that belief. Anyways, enough with the sentimental stuff, more about making money so that you can enjoy more experiences in this one life you have to live.

Estate sales are good opportunities for finding deals, but I've found that prices tend to be a little higher on items, especially if there's a third party that comes in to manage the sale. I've heard that third parties do their own price checks of some sort, which explains the less favorable pricing for us flippers.

Most estate sales I come across run three days in a row, from a Thursday through Saturday. You may get better deals on Saturday when they're trying to sell everything, but keep in mind that any of the really good items will likely be sold on the first or second day.

Clearance Racks and Holiday Sales

Clearance racks at department stores such as Wal-Mart and Target often have hidden gems at steep discounts. In addition to finding things on clearance racks, holiday sales offer many deals to consider. Personally, I have never been a big shopper. I try to steer clear of malls and crowds when it comes to Black Friday shopping or other holiday deals, although I know there is a lot of opportunity. If you're willing to stop by a few places on holidays, check out major discounts, and stock up on a few key items, you can easily resell for a profit online.

Once you find items you think you want to purchase, how do you know what to buy or how much you should pay? How do you know when you're getting a good deal, and what your potential profit can be when you mark items up? You should price check most items before you buy when possible. Chapter 2 discusses this in more detail.

Chapter 2: Price Check Before Purchasing

Before you buy anything, you should price check the item of interest on a few sources if possible. Check Craigslist, or maybe Amazon or eBay and see what the exact item or a similar item is selling for. Does it seem to be something popular? Or is it outdated and worth very little? If you find a keyboard, as in the musical instrument, for $30 and it's in good condition, you can be confident that you will turn a pretty profit.

I found this exact deal and bought on the spot, especially after seeing that the lowest offered price for the exact item (same brand and similar condition) was $150 on platforms like eBay or Facebook Marketplace. I ended up selling it so someone locally for $100 as I was happy enough with a $70 profit.

Items found at stores with barcodes will be easier to price check as you can use the Amazon Seller app or a barcode scanning app in general to see what the items are selling for online. Items found at garage or estate sales may be slightly more difficult to price check as there are usually no barcodes and items can even be completely unbranded. Examples of unbranded items include custom furniture or antiques.

It's best to price check whenever possible. This helps ensure that there will be enough potential profit margin built in to make the item worth your time. However, sometimes you may want to take calculated risks on random items that you can't price check from time to time.

A few "risks" I took on items include a vintage baseball bat, four men's suits, and five storage bins. I say "risks" because I hardly spent much money in buying the items at all. I bought the baseball bat for $2, the suits for $8, and the storage bins for $5, making my total initial investment costs $15.

I sold the bat for $20 to someone who wanted to be Negan from The Walking Dead for Halloween and sold the storage bins for $25 total. So, I turned $15 into $45, profiting $30 even without even having sold any suits yet. I've had a few interested people for the suits, which I currently have priced at $60 per piece. If I can even sell the suits at $20 per piece, my profit jumps up by an additional $80. Low risk and a decent reward.

In most cases, you're buying these items at such a low price that if for any reason you're having a hard time selling, chances are you can at least break even and let your item go at the price you paid for it. I paid $2 per suit. Where the heck will you find a full two-piece suit for $2? Even the cheap ones found in department stores are at least $100+!

Now that you know about price checking or taking calculated risks, let's talk about getting your products into the hands of interested buyers.

Chapter 3: Selling Your Items

After you've stocked up on a few items that have ideally been price checked to estimate profit potential, it's time to post your items for sale. You're going to want to post on multiple platforms to maximize the number of eyes on the items.

I personally post to all or some of the following, depending on the type of item:

- Craigslist
- Facebook Marketplace
- Letgo
- eBay
- Amazon

Make sure to take great pictures of your products using a phone camera or a real camera if you have one. I have the Canon G7X and absolutely love it. It's nice having a real camera so that I don't have 10 pictures of some random item I'm selling taking up precious phone space.

For my personal workflow, I take photos on my camera, save them all to my Dropbox folder, and then post to all platforms of interest from my computer in most cases. Sometimes, I'll save the photos to my phone from Dropbox and post to Facebook Marketplace or Letgo directly from my phone if I'm away from the computer.

I try to post pictures of the items from every angle in a well-lit environment. You want to make sure that the items are clean or wiped down to make them presentable prior to taking your pictures as well.

Post a good, descriptive title and a detailed enough description to show buyers you've done your homework. Notice the difference in these two examples below, and think about which one would be more likely to get a positive response from a potential buyer.

<u>*Example A*</u>
Item:
- Shoes

Description:
- Shoes for sale, for men. Fits well.

Example B

Item:
- Arcertyx Hiking Shoes (Men's Size 12)

Description:
- I have a brand-new pair of Arcteryx hiking shoes that are in the original box and still have tags on them. They are yellow and are size 12 for men.
- These shoes have never been worn and are looking to "pair" with the right feet.

I'm hoping you picked Example B as the more legit one. And no, you don't have to include an eye-rolling pun in the description. Using a listing like Example B, I sold two pairs of shoes that I bought for $25 each on eBay for $120 each in just a few days (plus $10 for shipping).

Platform Pros and Cons

There are various platforms out there. Some cater primarily to local buyers (Facebook Marketplace, Craigslist, and Letgo) and the big ones allow you to access buyers from all over the country (eBay and Amazon).

When selling locally, use:
- Facebook Marketplace
- Craigslist
- Letgo

The pros of platforms catering to local buyers are that you can get cash for your flips immediately. You can ask buyers to meet at a location convenient to both of you and get the transaction done without any listing, packaging, or shipping fees.

The cons of these platforms are that you have a more limited buyer audience. If you have a niche item, it may be more difficult to find a seller in your exact area that wants it.

I tend to like to flip large items that are difficult to ship locally, such as bar stools or musical instruments. For items that are small and easy to ship, consider using the nationwide buyer platforms, eBay and Amazon.

To access more buyers, use:
- Amazon
- eBay

There are multiple pros of eBay and Amazon. Firstly, you have access to a larger audience. The two pairs of hiking shoes that I bought got sold to people in other states through eBay. I may have had to sit on the inventory for a longer amount of time if I was trying to find buyers in my city or surrounding areas. After all, Houston isn't the nation's best hiking spot.

Another pro is that these platforms are very buyer-friendly. Buyers trust the platforms and feel safe. They know that they can get their money back if there's any issues or a scammer puts up a fake listing.

There are a few cons to these platforms, however. For eBay, there are sometimes listing fees you must pay, even if your item ends up not selling. For both eBay and Amazon, you will have to pay a percentage of the selling price if the item sells. These fees can cut into your profit margin pretty significantly in some cases.

You will have to box and ship your items, which is not always a fun step when you're starting out. I've also run across several items that individual sellers are restricted from selling on Amazon, which means you may have to resort to other platforms.

Chapter 4: Order Fulfillment

The final stretch: order fulfillment. You're almost there!

eBay or Amazon Sales

If you've sold an item through a platform like eBay or Amazon, you'll have to pack and ship your product. Follow the steps outlined on those platforms. You can print out a barcode to put on your package or simply have a sticker put on the package at your local post office.

I've had the best rates and luck when shipping through the U.S. Postal Service. I find that using other carriers is often too pricey and cuts too deeply into profit margin.

USPS offers tracking for even the most basic shipments. You can upload tracking number when you confirm that you've shipped your product. The buyer receives that information and can track their package, and this is often times the point where funds are released to your account. Sometimes, you may have funds withheld for some time until product is delivered (this happened to me early on with my eBay account, but I received the money within a few days of shipping).

A quick word of caution: make sure to closely follow eBay's directions as scammers try to target new sellers (especially when you try to sell high ticket items). Their hope is that you'll ship them a product before they pay, and then you'll be out of luck once they end up not paying and disappearing.

Pro-tip: Send a follow-up email to buyers once they've received their products.

Write a short, nice email saying you hope everything went well and asking them to leave a short, positive review if they enjoyed the buying experience. If you added a nice note in the box and did a great job of packaging, they might take the extra minute to give you a good review.

Sales to local buyers

When selling to local buyers, you should obviously exercise caution. You're meeting with a stranger at a random location. You should try to pick a well-lit, public place and meet in daylight. I would avoid meeting people in a dark alley late at night with high-ticket items. It may be a good way to get robbed.

I haven't had any bad experiences meeting up with people in public, but I don't take chances. I have a Concealed Handgun License (CHL) and usually am locked and loaded with a 9mm in my inside-the-waistband holster. Again, I've had great experiences and met up with tons of really nice people. But I feel better about being able to potentially handle the situation if an attempted robbery or life-threatening situation were to arise.

The sketchy feeling mainly comes up from faceless connections, where you have absolutely no idea of who you're meeting up with. Facebook Marketplace offers a nice solution as you get messages from users with profiles. This allows you to do some investigation of your potential buyers.

I don't like to judge a book by its cover, but I do take a look at the interested person when they contact me via Facebook Messenger. I've ignored messages from people interested in buying a cell phone that have pictures of guns pointed at the camera, for example.

I suggest carrying some loose cash with you when meeting people. This way, you can make sure you have change if they have big bills to get the transaction completed. Once the sale is complete, don't forget to delete the listings so that you don't get messages from other interested buyers.

Pro-tip: Get buyers to meet at a location convenient to you.

My favorite deals are the ones where I leave my house five minutes before the agreed upon time, meet with a buyer at a location close to me, and come straight home with my pocket full of extra cash. Gas stations seem to work well as they're well lit, populated, and usually conveniently located.

Chapter 5: Tracking Profits and Progress

I suggest using an Excel file to track your progress. I have an Excel "FlipLog" file that I created to stay on top of my numbers. I can automatically update charts and graphs after entering in some manual information and clicking "refresh."

I make a list of all the items I have purchased and have several columns of information. One column shows the price I paid for each item. Another column shows what I think I can sell the items for based on my price check. Yet another column displays my actual sell price. Finally, a summary column calculates my profits after subtracting out any costs such as packaging or shipping that I may have incurred.

I'm able to see a summary highlighting my net profit overall. You obviously want to have this number be positive, where your wins greatly outweigh any losses. Remember the example I talked about earlier, where I turned $15 into $45, more than covering my initial investment.

Sometimes, you may take risks and sit on inventory that is slightly more expensive and takes longer to sell, but remember that chances are, you can probably at least break even and sell for what you bought it at if you really want to.

Chapter 6: Negotiation Tips

Negotiating While Buying Items

When you find items that you want to buy, keep a poker face on. Try not to show excitement or interest when you come across items that you really want, or you will abandon your bargaining power. Play it cool as if you don't really care and are just browsing around. Note that this only works at garage or estate sales. You probably won't get very far with negotiating price at a department store.

If you've discovered something you think could be profitable over a long period of time, come up with a believable story of why you need the items. When I came across a cell phone store that was getting rid of a bunch of bus boxes, which basically look like TSA containers at the airport, I had purchased five because they were $1 each.

I posted them for $5 dollars each later that night and had five people message me on Facebook Marketplace within 10 minutes. I immediately realized that this was an item that was in high demand and I could charge more for. I also discovered that Amazon had the exact same brand listed for $18 each.

I went back to the store the next day to buy all the containers that I could squeeze into my Honda Accord. I managed to fit 77 more containers into my car and purchased them on the spot. Instead of telling the store owner that I had success selling them at $5 per piece, I mentioned that a friend was looking to purchase several containers for low-cost for his own store.

I am not a fan of lying, but in these situations with sellers where it's just a five-minute, one-time conversation, it can be better not to disclose your true intentions in order to maximize your profit potential. A worst-case scenario would be if you told the store owner that you easily sold all of them for $5 per piece and he changed his mind last minute, making the price $5 per unit or limiting the amount you can purchase at one time. In those cases, the deal would no longer be as appealing for you.

Negotiating While Selling Items

When I'm listing an item, I usually start with a very high price that is borderline ridiculous. I do this on all platforms but sometimes try different prices on different platforms to see if I get any bites.

When I start by listing prices high, I have a chance to potentially have a really big profit. If nobody seems interested at the initial high price points I set, I simply reduce prices slightly weekly or every few days. Eventually, if you have an item that is in demand, you will find a buyer.

Facebook Marketplace will even show buyers when the seller has lowered the price by displaying the previous price with a strikethrough. This helps pique their interest as they feel like they are getting a better deal than they would have initially. Another benefit of listing prices high is that you can negotiate with someone to "meet in the middle." For example, let's say you want to sell an item for $200. You should post at a number slightly higher than what you really want, because rarely does someone pay the exact price listed without some negotiation.

Here's an example of how the conversation will most likely go:

Example: Selling a musical keyboard. You would be happy with $200, so you list the item at $230.

Buyer: "Hi, I'm interested in your item. My offer is $170 for the keyboard.

Seller: "Hi, thanks for your message. Sorry, I cannot lower the price that significantly. Could you do $210?"

Buyer: "I only have $200 right now, can you do that deal?"

Seller: "Okay, I can do $200. Can you meet me at ABC parking lot at 3:00pm today?"

Buyer: "That works for me, I will see you then."

Notice how the seller offers $210 in the first round of negotiations. You might be surprised at how many times this actually works. The buyer may be happy that you have "easily" conceded and lowered your number, and take that offer. If the buyer does try to go even lower, you still have wiggle room built into the price to work with and are able to offer a second reduced price to get them to the amount that you actually wanted in the first place ($200 in this example).

If you look like you're willing to work with the buyer and drop the price for them, they'll be more willing to drive further out of their way to meet you at a location convenient to you.

I have taken college classes on psychology and even on negotiations, but it's so much more amazing when you see the principles in the works. People like getting good deals and love buying, but they hate feeling ripped off. If you can provide an offer that looks like an amazing deal to them, you will maximize your profits.

Imagine selling the $200 keyboard in this example when you paid $50 for it at a garage sale. Assuming you sell locally and don't have to pay listing or shipping fees, that's a $150 profit. Now, imagine if the next cheapest keyboard for sale (assuming that it's the exact same model and in similar condition) online is selling for $300. You could mark yours up to $250 and still have the best deal for the buyer.

Pro-tip: Bundle cheap items in with more expensive items to sweeten the deal.

If you are trying to sell more premium items and the buyer is unsure, try to throw in a related item that is not worth much to you. For example, I've sold two bar stools at a higher price by throwing in a nightstand that I purchased for just $5 at a garage sale.

Chapter 7: Ready, Set, Flip

There are risks that must be undertaken in order to reap rewards. You won't make any profits if you don't buy inventory. You sometimes have to buy things based on a gut feeling when there are no good price checks available online. Take risks, take action, and make profits. You'll learn as you go and you'll get better each time you do it.

I've had some poor choices on items where I've sat on inventory for weeks, ultimately selling at about the price I bought the items at. But on average, I've profited hundreds of dollars a month with just a few hours of my time. In fact, I usually only go on my garage or estate sale hunts one or two Saturdays a month while I'm out running errands. I work a few sales into my itinerary and spend no more than a few hours on it.

While I'm driving to sales, I'm listening to an audiobook or podcast, making my time completely productive. After stopping by a few sales, I head to the gym to get a workout in, and maybe get some work done at a coffee shop while I wait for a buyer to meet me to make a purchase. I then smile as I sip on my coffee which is paid for with the profit from my sale.

I get other business work done, make another sale or two, and head home to take pictures and put up posts for my new products from that day's garage sale finds. That's where the flipping work stops until I get a new message from another interested buyer. If I don't get messages after a few days, I lower the price and play the waiting game once more.

Results don't just happen. You've got to put in the time and the work. Follow these guidelines and add your own in based on your successes. This book is your "diet" and your "workout plan" that will help you grow your flipping muscles *when and only when you take action.*

Start off with lower priced items to get your feet wet and work yourself up to the pricier items with larger profit margins. As you grow in success rate and confidence, you can take greater risks. You can even limit yourself in the beginning to only purchase items to flip using profits from previous flips. This way, you ensure that you're never risking too much.

Now get out there, and start applying everything you've learned. Remember that knowledge is not power. Execution is power!

About the Author

Chris Bello is a serial entrepreneur based in Houston, Texas. He is the Co-Founder of Flexthetics, where he and a childhood friend invented a supplement organizer product. He also consults with individuals in need of supply chain advice or life motivation in general.

In his free time, Chris enjoys exercising, playing the drums, and traveling. He is a strong believer of "experiences over things" and tries to live life to the fullest every single day. A testament to this lifestyle is the fact that he is both skydive and scuba certified.

Less dreaming, more doing. Reach Chris with questions or comments at www.chrisbello.com.